THE PEOPLE YOU LEFT BEHIND.

Embracing the loss of a loved one and living with it

STACY MURDOCK

INTRODUCTION

When confronted with the sudden death of a loved one, we are thrown into a spiral of diverse emotions. The death of a loved one is not something we are prepared for, even when the signs are there. There's a fickle of hope we hold onto, hoping, believing that they will live through it.

But then things do not always go as we plan, our hopes are shattered right before our eyes and we are faced with a pain so immense it seems like it is the end for us.

How do we cope with loss of a loved one? How do we keep living and experiencing life even though we feel like we are left behind?

This is a book for the people who feel left behind; this is a book for those going through unbearable pain. I hope you find comfort as you slip through the pages of this book.

CHAPTER ONE

A BLAND TUESDAY AFTERNOON

Nothing prepares you for the loss of someone precious to you; someone whom you hold dear to your heart, with whom you have shared beautiful, ugly and in between memories with. Nothing prepares you for that moment when you will be separated from a person who is a constant, reliable person in your life, especially when you think you still have more time to spend with them. I personally dread the suddenness of losing someone who I believe to be always there every time I look over my shoulder. One minute everything is in harmony, you have plans to spend some quality time together and the next minute, you are left in shock of a sudden bitter reality, the person you love and adore is no more breathing.

This translates to a variety of feelings for most of us, especially when the deceased person is a major intricate part of our lives. Is it humanly possible to love someone so dearly, without that person becoming a major part of your life? So here you are staring at a bland Tuesday afternoon, even with the sun shining and people going about their respective lives totally oblivious of your shock, the sun has stopped shining for you.

We all experience grief in different degrees, some of us we become suddenly numb to everything and everyone around us, the pain of the reality of loss hits with a magnitude so strong we feel like our worlds have fallen apart. The problem here is that no one can understand our loss exactly the way we feel it, loss is a unique individual experience for each of us. So when our loved ones show care and say kind and well-meaning words to sooth our aching hearts, the sad truth is, it doesn't make us feel better. Maybe we are distracted from our pain when they come around to comfort us, But then the pain always remain there, days roll into weeks, and weeks into months and it is still a bland ordinary day

Some of us wonder how they expect us to move on from the blandness we see which obviously they cannot see, you hear words like everything happens for a reason, maybe life is teaching you a lesson, there's meaning to this pain you are experiencing at the moment, our friends and families say all these well meaning words to help most times, the problem is it doesn't help. Everything is bland. Nothing said will change anything. Neither can life be restored to our loved ones.

So here we are in our bland planet. Here every day is just another day the words and actions of the people around us, who try to care, fade into nothingness. And while we are here, our loved ones worry because we have little or too much interest in food. We say nothing or scream obscenities. Our therapists are beckoning us to move on and we look at them wondering if there was a manual for experiencing grief, because if there was, I bet we would all grab a copy to find answers to all the questions running in our heads which constitutes this blandness we cannot seem to get over.

CHAPTER TWO

QUESTIONS

The first word that left my mouth in the midst of my shock was WHY? Why was my beloved in an accident? Why him? He was a good person, a kind and affectionate partner, my best friend, a leader, the kindest man the world has ever experienced. And many more questions followed. How did it happen? What were his last thoughts before he gave up? Was he in pain? Did he think of me? Did he try to escape? What if I had forced him to have his vehicle serviced when he made that offhand comment of his brakes failing last week? Why did he have to experience such intensity of pain?

Questioning is an unavoidable process of grief. The pain that accompanies grief is instant, not easily dismissed, and it doesn't give us a chance to prepare. So we question it? Our humanity questions everything and everyone around us? Why are we forced to experience such degree of pain without our permission or preparation? Why is life cruel to us? Is there anything we can do to stop feeling pain? Does wanting to stop our pain make us bad or selfish people? Should we not be grateful instead? But how can we be grateful for the pain we feel? Do we really need to feel pain and loss to gain a better perspective on life? We wonder why people tell us that we would get a deeper meaning in life from the pain we are feeling. Is pain the only path to a deeper meaning in life?

We ask questions because we are built to search for answers always in the midst of our chaos. We ask questions because cannot comprehend the pain that has being forced upon us, maybe we have felt pain before but I believe there are degrees to the kind of pain we experience. The pain we experience from losing a cell phone isn't the same as losing a child that went to college. And for each of us, the way we respond to our grief is unique.

I personally believe that asking questions while grieving is normal and healthy, because in asking questions we will find answers to our pain. These answers may not necessarily be solutions to making our pain stop or put an end to our grief, rather it is finding comfort and courage to live with the reality of our loss.

CHAPTER THREE

BREAKTHROUGHS AND DOWNS

I thought I was on the edge of my breakthrough, I finally got back to my job, I began to laugh at funny jokes from my colleagues, Smith had being laid to rest six months ago and my friends were happy I was living again. I started work, went grocery shopping, cooked , ate, sorted my bills, watched my favorite TV shows, even my therapist was proud of my progress until it all went down in a spiral all over again. The problem here is I have convinced myself I had moved on from grief, I believed I was staring at the light at the end of the tunnel; it was supposed to get brighter from here. But then it hit me all over again, this time even worse than the first time, it felt like opening a fresh wound all over again and the pain this time felt like a tornado.

We often feel a spiral of emotions when it comes to grieving. A breakdown, when you think you have overcome the pain of grief is normal. The problem for most of us is our attempt to cure grief. Grief is not a disease that should be cured. It is not an aliment to get rid of. It is not a disease you wake up, free of, after days of constant care, medications and all. One of the faults in our cultures is the underlying intent to cure grief. We forget that grieving is not a disease to be cured, but it is a natural response to loss. Grief is different for different people, there's no specified time to get over grief: grief is not something to get over; it is a natural response to loss which should be accepted, felt and validated.

I was so confused and angry all over again and couldn't quite understand why I was going through the pain of losing my partner again. I felt selfish, my loved ones had gone through a lot of sacrifices to get me back on the living again wheel, but here I was feeling worse than before with absolutely no explanation for it. I felt like I should, explain my grief, why I was back at square one when I should be on the front line, comforting those who were grieving and sharing my story to encourage them. I should have moved on by now, I mean I was doing just fine before out of nowhere I saw myself spiraling back into the dark alley of pain, depression, anxiety and all the siblings of grief.

I really wanted to be fine, so for days I pretended, lived a charade and put up a really good show of being alright. I wasn't going to put my loved ones through another long period of worrying about me and taking care of me. How selfish can you be? I asked myself for countless times while staring in the mirror. How selfish can you be?

The truth is I never really got around putting on appearances for so long, soon it was just too much to keep my breakdown tucked in, and my supposed breakthrough from grief was a breakdown waiting to happen. And when it finally overwhelmed me, I lost it all over again and this time, it was worse than it ever was.

CHAPTER FOUR

IS ANYONE THERE?

Is there a manual on how to go through grief? Are there regulations on what to expect? How you will feel? What to do to make it better? If there was, then I want a copy right now!!!

It takes someone who has truly loved to experience loss they say, if you don't love, then there's nothing to lose.

I feel lost and alone in this alley of pain, even when I find words to explain how I feel to the people around me, the look on their faces, displays confusion and misunderstanding. Even after I tell them severally of how much pain I am in, they all try to do the same thing: console me out of the pain, tell me it would get better with time, some of them try to make jokes to make me feel better and all of these makes me realize just how lonely I am in all of this.

If I had a way, I would love to meet another person who is in this alley of pain like me, who knows exactly the way I feel and can understand the magnitude of the burden I am carrying around. I would feel relieved to be understood for once.

Feeling alone in our grief even amongst our loved ones and those who care about us is something we cannot run from, even in a family where one person passes away, the individual members of the family respond to grief in their own unique way, no one person feels the magnitude of emotion same way as the other person. Hence the tendency to feel alone or singled out in a family of grieving people is a normal response to grief.

Some individuals might feel that their family members who are experiencing the same loss as them do not understand how they really feel. Some even judge their family members because they feel that their family members are moving on too fast, or coping so well with grief while they themselves are unable to assemble the pieces of their life together.

The truth is that no one can comprehend exactly how we feel about our loss, even if we explain it a million times, but still we can find closure in those who care about us in order to learn to accept the finality of losing a loved one. The person who is lost is gone and trying to adjust to a life without that person is hard, notwithstanding how much we try. But if we really look, we will find somebody who may not feel exactly as we feel but will be willing to hold our hands as we navigate our way through grief.

CHAPTER FIVE

FIRST ATTEMPT AT MOVING ON

Moving on from the loss of a loved one is a fairy tale, it is like saying that you are wiping your slate clean of the existence of that person and no matter how hard we try, the existence of that person has become a part of our lives, and even when the person is no longer there, we cannot completely forget that person. There will things that will remind us, of the person who has shared life with us.

Grief is not something we move away from, distancing ourselves from it. Instead the right approach should be, coming to terms with the truth of the reality that a loved one has passed on, accepting it and learning to live with it.

Accepting the truth of the loss of a loved one is not easy, and having to live life without that person takes a lot of effort and courage. Because, every day, without our consent most times, there's always a reminder. Shared memories, shared hobbies, their favorite music, a celebrity they adore, their perfume worn by a stranger who ran into you, their favorite meme, their death anniversary and so many more. And even as the years go by, we are always reminded of our loss in one way or the other.

Like I said earlier, our best perspective, when dealing with of the loss of a loved one, is to understand the magnitude of the pain we are experiencing, and to understand our pain we must accept it. Accepting our pain means harmonizing with the pain as it rends our hearts apart, validating every bit of it even when it is so hard to do. The easier thing to do most times is to run away from our pain, try to do anything to shut it out and pretend to be fine, but the more we shut out our pain, the more it holds us down and destroys us from the inside. To understand our pain we must accept it, and to accept it we must feel every bit of it no matter how hard it is.

When we have harmonized with our pain despite its magnitude, it is then possible to understand and live with it.

Living with our pain doesn't mean it goes away, instead we are able to continue living while carrying our pains with us, but because we have understood and accepted our pain for what it is, we live and approach life not from bitterness because of the hurt we feel, but with grace, courage and effort. And as much it is easy to say in writing, it is very hard to practice and implement. It takes tremendous effort to move forward and chose to live life despite the pain we feel in our hearts. It takes one step, one day at a time to keep living.

CHAPTER SIX

YOU ARE DOING JUST FINE

In my previous chapters, I asked if there was a manual for grief. And right here, I would answer that, there is no manual for grief. Yes, there are people around us who has experienced loss, and listening to them tell you stories of how they felt when they were faced with the loss of their loved ones, can make you feel like you are not the only one who has experienced loss, but still it doesn't equate to your loss or make the pains of your loss disappear.

Accepting of the fact, that each of us responds uniquely to our emotions generally, and to grief is the key. The need to compare ourselves to other people when we feel we are still stuck in the web of our pain is compelling and it is important to understand that comparing ourselves to others will only make things even worse than it really is.

There is no specified time written anywhere, to grieve over the death of a loved one. Some people undergo a transformation that would last for the rest of their life after the death of a loved one, and other people also might not.

It is important that we understand that our individual feelings and response to grief are valid, and no matter how bad we feel and how stuck we feel, we are doing just fine. Waking up and choosing to live each day takes courage and a strong will to execute. It takes bravery to live each day and not take an easy way out. It takes courage to decide to keep living even when our loved one who made living so wonderful is no more.

Feeling really great for a couple of days and feeling all depressed is normal, finding yourself feeling angry on a beautiful day when everyone else is happy is normal, not even being able to explain or understand your emotions is also normal. We should learn to give ourselves the grace we would kindly extend to others. While we navigate through our feeling of grief and loss, we should learn to accept our emotions as we experience every one of them, we should try not to compare our progress with others or worse of all try to stifle our emotions and pretend to be fine.

No matter how hard it may seem, or how much of how at loss we might feel, that we are not progressing at living, with the reality of the loss of a loved one, let us always remember that we are doing just fine by deciding to live each day, and as we choose to accept, understand and live with the pain in our heart, it becomes easier to live and become all that we want to be.

We are the people they left behind and we are doing just fine as we keep understanding, accepting and becoming all we are meant to be.

www.ingramcontent.com/pod-product-compliance
Lightning Source LLC
Chambersburg PA
CBHW052139150726
48002CB00006B/2673